l'appel du vide

poems by

Kym Cunningham

Finishing Line Press
Georgetown, Kentucky

l'appel du vide

ACKNOWLEDGMENTS

A few of the poems in this chapbook have been previously published
elsewhere. "'see you next tuesday'" was published in Poetry Quarterly.
"Vegetable Temporal" will be published in *Best Emerging Poets of California*.
"Cannibalism is the Sincerest Form of Flattery" will be published in *Nasty
Women Poets: An Unapologetic Anthology of Subversive Verse*. A previous
version of "In Nomine Filii" was published by Zingara Poet. A previous
version of "It's not necessarily the Meth" was published in *Claudius Speaks*.

Publisher: Leah Maines
Editor: Christen Kincaid
Cover Art: Rebecca Cunningham
Author Photo: Ernest Chavez
Cover Design: Elizabeth Maines McCleavy

Printed in the USA on acid-free paper.
Order online: www.finishinglinepress.com
          also available on amazon.com

Author inquiries and mail orders:
Finishing Line Press
P. O. Box 1626
Georgetown, Kentucky 40324
U. S. A.

Table of Contents

for those who would have burned at the stake

Pied Piper

I stuck my tongue
down boys' throats
to keep them from speaking
They were beautiful
all-iron jawlines, glass cheekbones, and
country-club smiles

Their words made me want to ram
my head against the windshield
until it bled, but instead
I saw their
bets and raised them
my shirt

Keep up with me boys
never—keep up—
have I ever regretted
shaving myself bare
wearing too much eyeliner
eating the hearts
of those who loved me

I was not meant to live
in passenger's seats
I take off my shorts
to see theirs—too quick—I leave
I'm well-rehearsed
in disappearing
It's never as hard as I want it to be

The question remains
will I take them down with me
Expecting Helen
I can only yield Circe
The fall is sweeter
than their blood in my teeth
I never had the stomach for impact

meat

the smell of beef stew reminds us
of cold winds pressed against the bridge of our nose
our lips frosting car windows
as we watched his hands tremble
expectantly
cut the line
roll the dollar bill
hand it to us first
—always the gentleman—
we lean over the mirror on the dashboard
hair tucked behind our ears
like over microscopes in biology class
his eyes flick to our red twine thong
sausages greying in the twilit cold
we smile
our nose ringing
his hands going to the button on his pants
he is so beautiful, we believe
trying to cook ourselves
knowing we are already dead

Bored Out

She's a queen
Burger King crown
& cellophane evening gown
our Babylonian whore with rotten speech
—I was a knockout when I was young
broke men's hearts in a look—

You want to believe her
You can almost see
the sex appeal if only
you peeled away her skin
splayed her open
plucked at the fibers

You look for the past as you give her a tenspot to
bend over & clutch the dumpster
her frayed skirt hiked past hips
born from too many crystal-laced abortions
Recycling is messy

It's not necessarily the Meth

I played dental hygienist to a lion,
looking for onions between
red and black fjords but finding
a soulless cavern.

I knew the mouth;
I'd witnessed that decay before,
calcium crumbling
in the flash of a smirk.

That first mouth thought
I was fluoride,
but this mouth knew
I was just another set of teeth,
gingivitis already settling in.

Cannibalism Is the Sincerest Form of Flattery

You want to look
at my heavy bottom   lip
You wish
for a quiver
to give

I want
to lick fear
from your eyes

You whimper

Call me something
harder & mean it

You say you
cannot look away from
my father's eyes

Look away

I'm too pretty to be
so angry

What do you know
about control?

My jaw works words
like colors
flaying skin open

Bobbitt missed a step

Let me eat
your organs
smear my womb
with your iron-wrought power

Vegetable Temporal

I scratch my spine
where time
has taken root

He dips memory in honey
offering nostalgia
on hummingbird wings

My nails
dig outward
as blood blurs

the mirror and
I become slick
against my palms

He smiles
content among my vertebrae
nestled in between

columns that could rival
Greece or Rome
if only they would

apply themselves
If I had
X-ray vision

I could see
—if only
if I—

Kipling didn't know
the first thing
about regret

LA A(r)mor

You've been alive too long when traffic sounds
like the ocean and cars pass in heat waves
life stalled in the fast lane

You marry a man for his hipbones
You should've been a country singer
You weren't always so sharp

You look like easy prey
trying to fish winter from your bones
with laudanum and dead skin

You breathe just keep swimming
holding your mantra in positive pools
that choke you like flat champagne

Your throat-back gurgles
You jab a pencil in your neck
rummaging for clean air

Manson was half-right
Blood can be as powerful as bleach to wash
sin from our feet

We will always have Machu Picchu

I fell in love with a man who played guitar with his hand
against my throat, eyes closed, one Achilles tucked
behind another.
He crooned Spanish songs of violence.
His voice broke
in sharp mountain angles
as his cheekbones smoldered
against obsidian.

I knew I lost when I saw tears
cradled in the four moles beneath his eye.
I smelled him
in October winds:
unfiltered sunlight,
but I was drawn to the
cold current underneath.

definition

your amygdala fires and that means
he's cheating on you
paranoia is just a symptom of narcissism
a different pronoun explains staring at your nipples
you look at the skylight to keep from crying
you wish you could throw up but your stomach's
running on two hydrogens, one oxygen
your mouth tastes like saltines
you'd sacrifice a pound of flesh
to taste every molecule of history
at least then you'd know
which was worse
the symptoms
or the condition

Afterbirth

We are ragged at the edges, unrefined and stucco in hospital white
paper thoughts, like walls of our cardboard house
where you first took me
and I screamed, Murder!
I pushed my nose against your pulse
to smell lost memories
You had been with me always
But silence breaks the umbilical cord
and your breasts aren't where I put them
You stick your hand down my sewer grate and
whisper, Take the thorn leave the rose!

Critical Thinking

If there is a line between art and madness
could you open the sky in my cleft of hair
could I peel you back to see blood
could you separate your sperm from my mud

If happiness is always blind
should we roll on the floor like leaves
should we look through the two-way mirror
should we leave our bodies here

If I were to die tonight
would you still feel me in the back of your spine
would I live as that light pressing against your eye
would you be solvent enough to say goodbye

Death Is Never Far Away

You were born in smoke free from fire—
the reminder hanging above
this city like a shroud

Your eyes stream with the ocean—
salt-pearls collecting in visible
folds of skin

You feel disjointed—
a body too separate
to be at rest

You taste heartbreak more than love
You drown in ghosts
Your mouth will never be cold again

fucking junkies

it's the cheekbones
so clear you'd swear they were made of glass
the hair cut like mirrors that make you
lick the stale sweat from their bodies
push your fingers into rings beneath their eyes
massage bruises
turn green to purple and end with black
run your fingerprints over dead veins
arms like the roots of some great tree
feet never ticklish
they've tasted death
kissed themselves goodbye
the closest to beasts you're still allowed to fuck
how could anyone resist

In Nomine Filii

The walnut man in a broken straw hat
divined our future in streetside palm fronds:
the house on oil-derrick stilts and
that three-legged dog I always
wanted. Baby, our children
would be beautiful if only they had
none of me and all of you.
Your hair, your smile.
Your lips, your eyes.
Your skin. But I can't
let them be broken, too. So
every month, I split an egg;
watch the yolk lick
down my legs. We fall
asleep to dreams of
monsters singing praises
of our mercy.
Tell me, Love,
are we thicker
than water?

even Saturn will Return

There comes a point in any great relationship where you look across dinner and think—I could kill you now, pick up that pen and stab it through your throat, loop those headphones around your neck and pull, just for a second, quick enough for a kiss.

That's how you know you love him—isn't it—when you fantasize death.

If you didn't love him, you wouldn't be able to feel him past your heart, scratching at the lining of your small intestine. You wouldn't question if you were culpable in his existence, you wouldn't think you'd all be better off dead.

You feel salt slip down your cheek. He looks at you and asks— what's wrong.

You wipe yourself away. Nothing—you say—just dust.

Hunger

You said I was unfit
for human consumption
that promises had spoiled me
saturating my skin with
lies neither of us could keep

I don't want to be our escaped goat
bucking at the slaughter
I don't want you to
disembowel me like tree fruit
letting my seeds dehisce your mouth

I never said I could be selfless
I never said I had the answers
I never said I'd give you my life
let you churn me up, skim me alive
spread me on soured dough

But you've left me out and
the butter's curdled, the jam's attracting flies
you've begun to mold
one of us must clarify
we can't trick the starving into eating us anymore

"see you next tuesday"

he was asking for it
wearing that three-piece suit

i couldn't help myself

he told me to smile and i
shoved my fist down his throat
until he tasted anger

sorry officer
you are neither judge nor jury
but your fury blinds you to me

you claim not to see black and white
but they exist to make you hear resist
and perceive my body
as a threat

i've been called worse things

by any other name

i am not patient
i am not kind
i am envious boastful proud
i dishonor others

i seek myself

i anger easily
i keep a list of those who have wronged me
i rejoice in evil

i do not trust because i see
i do not hope because i know

i persevere where everything else fails
i am the prophesy
i will not cease

The fourth in a line of six children, **Kym Cunningham** had the unique opportunity of growing up in many places, realizing early on that most locales—and people—are the same. She was born just outside of Washington DC, although her family only stayed there for three years before moving to Helsinki, Finland. Unfortunately, she remembers very little Finnish, which she keeps meaning to remedy. One of her favorite memories involves looking at prehistoric paintings in Finnish caves, after which she swears she saw an elusive Saimaa seal, one of the few freshwater seals in the world—a memory that no one in her family has been willing to corroborate.

Forever intrigued by the misunderstood, Kym has been obsessed with wolves since the third grade; her parents and siblings supported her bizarre and, at times, unnerving fixation, showering her with gifts of various lupine paraphernalia. Kym was specifically fascinated by the paradox wolves represent: at once the genetic equivalent to man's best friend as well as the target of zealous eradication crusades. Upon learning the egregious lengths American settlers went to exterminate wolves, Kym was introduced to the thoughtless cruelty inherent within Euro-American colonialism.

As an angsty teenager and later as an emerging intellectual, Kym made a point of criticizing American neocolonial culture, possibly because she never really felt like she fit in, anyway. As a result, her poems usually read with much more cruelty and venom than she originally intended or even really feels.

Regardless of her previous locational infidelity, she has decided that she belongs in California, after first moving to the University of San Diego for her bachelors in English and history. She spent four years in the sun and then had the absurd idea that she could acclimate to the arctic of Boston, where it snowed from October until June. She left very soon thereafter, packing her life into a tiny hatchback and driving at breakneck speeds to the expatriated palm trees of San José. There, she received an MFA in creative nonfiction and poetry from San José State University and met her partner, Ernest. She and Ernest have since moved to Long Beach, where they live across from the Pacific with their adorably infuriating dog, Truffle Monster—the only child they will ever have.

www.ingramcontent.com/pod-product-compliance
Lightning Source LLC
LaVergne TN
LVHW021129080426
835510LV00021B/3362